OTHER POETRY COLLECTIONS BY DAVID GIANNINI

MAYHAP

Selected
Brief
Poems

David Giannini

DOS MADRES

2019

DOS MADRES PRESS INC.
P.O.Box 294, Loveland, Ohio 45140
www.dosmadres.com   editor@dosmadres.com

Dos Madres is dedicated to the belief that the small press is essential to the vitality of contemporary literature as a carrier of the new voice, as well as the older, sometimes forgotten voices of the past. And in an ever more virtual world, to the creation of fine books pleasing to the eye and hand.

Dos Madres is named in honor of Vera Murphy and Libbie Hughes, the "Dos Madres" whose contributions have made this press possible.

Dos Madres Press, Inc. is an Ohio Not For Profit Corporation and a 501 (c) (3) qualified public charity. Contributions are tax deductible.

Executive Editor: Robert J. Murphy

Illustration & Book Design: Elizabeth H. Murphy
www.illusionstudios.net

Typset in Adobe Garamond Pro & Lucida Bright
ISBN 978-1-948017-51-0
Library of Congress Control Number: 2019944625

First Edition

Published by Dos Madres Press, Inc.

ACKNOWLEDGEMENTS

Special thanks to Billie Chernicoff who suggested the title for this book; to Andrew Schelling for early readings of many of the poems; and especially to Pam Bachrach, always my first and most intuitive reader. I am also grateful to Elizabeth and Robert Murphy of Dos Madres Press who, with this book, have now published four volumes of mine.

Most of the poems in this book first appeared in the following publications, thanks to the editors:

Bongos (Japan), "Who Would Want To Be."

Cattails, "Somehow, The Impossible."

Clwn Wars (sic), "Vampyre."

Common Sense #5, "Two Views of Old Man in the Mountain."

Haiku Foundation, Per Diem Archive, April 2014 . ., "Last Sound." (published untitled, the poem beginning "His wristwatch.")

Hummingbird Magazine, "Abstract;" "Across Country;" "Barometer;" "February;" "Hammock;" "Jungian;" "Pathetic Fallacy" (under the title, "Lakeside;") "Leaves, Meaning

Leaves;" "Narcissus;" "No Small;" "Outpatient;" "Prospector/ Poet;" and "Washing the Sheets."

Lilliput Review, "For Don Wentworth" (both originally published without the present title;) and "After Five Days Rain."

Poets Who Sleep / Longhouse, " Orchard."

Longhouse accordion fold-out booklet, "Brothers;" "How Else?"

NOON: An Anthology of Short Poems, "A Jar."

Noon, journal of the short poem (Japan), "To See a World;" "A Jar;" "Humility;" "17 Syllables For N.A.S.A.'s Mars/MAVEN Project; "Drought;" "A Moment Before Breakfast."

Otata (online), "Another Springtime Future," "As Poetry Stalks You," "March," "Power Outage," "Somehow, the Impossible," and "To You, Reader."

Potlatcxh, Volume Two, "Flight" (originally without the final two lines.)

Stem, "Chestnuts."

NOTE: Some of the ancient poets came to believe life is poetry, and therefore daily, moment with moment, notes of birds and notes becoming poems. Cid Corman, with whom I corresponded for decades, often said, "Catch the poem as it is occurring." In that spirit, I offer the brief, fugitive pieces in this book as more or less an anthology with one author.

Little bit by little bit, we fix the day.

—Joanne Kyger

*That each leaf comes from a
threatened tree*

—Andrew Schelling

TABLE OF CONTENTS

To You, Reader

Do you really think
you won't have to pause
and savor silence before
and after these words?

And after such silence
(as your eyes lift from the page)
won't you need to become
what you have to say?

Two Views of The Old Man in the Mountain

Franconia, New Hampshire, 1979,
before *The Old Man* cracked off.

1.

There are granites and waters of the human face—
in love fantastic routes come fresh
as air around the eagle's outstretched wings.

2.

When we do not love we are like this
keeper of stone routes
firred from the neck down
occasional for the touring eye
good only as the silence following old nests.

Who Would Want to Be

you—Sisyphus—pushing
hopelessly ever—as if to
become the very rock—not
what the mountain wants.

Narcissus

Try to stand before
a mirror and not

see you but man as
man staring at an

other. Come to think
of it: open-eyed

kindness to strangers
seeks heart in each—or

is vanity too
fast even for glass?

Chestnuts

Toys. Dry hearts
of my father's childhood.
Thumbtips
fallen around *his* father's
grave. I keep
searching for some
green in their spiked husks.
Perhaps my brother
combing from another
direction,
will be there
in the tree.

Brothers

We find us
feeling found
to each other
again:

four brothers

at the casket
of our father—
holding on-
to the rain.

Father

His wristwatch
still ticking
the casket.

No Small

It is no small thing
    to breathe in the dark, to feel
memories smell of light,
    but only if our bodies,
sensing old time,

    open benign interiors
and catch the cached faces
    of our dead, only then
can we know in the dark
    true smiles have no wills.

Forest Floor

For Robert Murphy

Who can't lift
that flat box
of moonlight

will witness

its contents
rising in
another.

Two for Don Wentworth

Sunbeams

      so much we didn't hear

          until they fell.

=========

Old tree

      breaks slowly

          from its fruit.

After Five Days' Rain

Clouds
tear around the sun

or is it sun
tears through? Take

your pick—be
light about it too.

Jungian

for Cid

Say we know
yet it comes
down to this:

the shadow
of the grass-
hopper also
            leaps.

Eleven Intuitive Measures
(On Poetry / Poets)

*Poems are not made out of ideas. They are
made out of words.*

— Stéphane Mallarmé

1. *Riddle: All Poets Moving In A Circle. . .*

The honor
is to come
after them

until they
come after
you again.

2. *Ars. . .*

for Janet MacFadyen

As if from a type of rain once,
then rill and brook, river and sea
with sun and moon, even
minor as a flurry comes to be,
poetry comes and comes again
until we wake in the rush
of waters within—
friend, no flood needs praise.

Discipline makes the words come to,
as if from coma, coming to be as they come
within the discipline that makes you making
them and your life as one, the possible
not always arriving from great distance,
yet always from the stars
because we are from same, even so
for the waters before they had names.

3. *As Poetry Stalks You. . .*

To be initially uncertain, or only as certain completely submerged desert lizards can swim through sand to escape some surged predator known, not seen, but sensing you to catch and ever so slowly devour, almost as ion with ion, as glass dissolving in water—to remember as you attempt to sing: keep your vowels close and your consonants closer:

Wop-bop-a-loo-mop-alop-bom-bom.

4. *Prospector / Poet. . .*

Always to be
  at the top of
    your buddle
      watching
       waste
         reveal
           ore.

5. *Someone Writes, Say,*

of old cloth
and fine bedding—but watch out
for certain poets bearing stiffs:

where they lie,
though the thread count is high,
the starch is unbearable.

6. *Organic , Hairy. . .*

Out of the treetops endlessly rocking
her peek-peek, her rattle and whinny,
the up and come of her beak
knocks on wood. Similar

and dissimilar to the first words in the first
line of a poem seeking what is not
already known: peck-peck, the thing to be
found through the journey.

7. *To try. . .*

to keep your ear and eye to the ages
and hope that something you write
is sound
            outside of Time; to assay
all in the scales of your own authenticity,
the poem in its last line to feel destined.

8. *Remembrance Is Covert Poetics. . .*

Old black
notebook of blank
pages flipping

back to all they were
in the upright forest
before saws.

9. *Simon Says. . .*

Your job in the world is to find
as much poetry as possible
but this
        is not easy

for the frauds of perception leap with bouquets

as you swerve in the dark with the bituminous smell
of fresh paving on planet X
                with its crossroads
                        and steep
curves—nevertheless
                as you watch and listen:
Simon says
do this.

10. *Somehow, The Impossible. . .*

To Ed Baker in an email, and now in memoriam

To meet the maze in
the Minotaur and not

the other way 'round, Ed,
is poetry—step up

and step to—collapse
stone walls and

breathe through
your horns!

11. *Postscript: The Perfumist. . .*

Well slam my glove if he don't risk
being just another piss-poor poet
trying to make scents at least
of all truthful things more or less

like a deodorant puck in a urinal.

Abstract

for Julio Granda

Broken wing—no scream—
but the naïve agony
of shadow
        shatters.

Flight

Your night-
   gown limp on
the peg
   as it
always is
   by day,
but you
   are away—
3000 miles
   and a week
from here—
   breeze
lifting your hem.

Citizens!

Because spiritual fascists and killers dress
like patriots, death
stands in our pupils—until they witness
a promised land depends upon its premises.

Vampyre

Darkness the size
of yourself—
climb in.

Outpatient

Listening
all day to
others'
sadnesses—

we come
home so
much more
to the sun.

Cervantes

What if
it is him

(Miguel)
being

truly
blind to

windmills &
ways of wind

but he pens
& pins the

tale on the Don
Qui....?

To See a World

Only a grain
of sand riding
a grain of sand

        or is it the dream
        of a first stone step-
        ping up to glisten?

17 Syllables for N.A.S.A.'s Mars / Maven Project

We give each other
space knowing infinity's
the last of its kind.

Pathetic Fallacy

Skip it!—
      even stone
           has the right
               to commit
                    euphoria.

A Moment Before Breakfast

Reflected
as in any metal spoon
your face upside-down

placed
into your mouth
(metallic

taste) then
withdrawn blurred
wet-faced

revenant of
reflection
lampoon of spit

and wee pillages
of torpor
all there is.

Washing the Sheets

We are
born into
breath to be

borne as
(I thought
Pam said)

the shouts
are
drying.

Vision

Up
on
a
hill
looking
ahead at my
tracks already
there as if
begging
me
to
catch
up

Drought

A woven
basket on the flat public lot

in wind makes

suspicious improvisations
topsy-turvy

        topples to

someone petitioning the sky
to be in love with thunder.

Barometer

for Jane Laning

The web
shudders   doesn't tear
in this wind/rain   and the master
knows this   (do you understand?)   she
knows and before any storm   spider tightens
her rigging   captain-&-crew as one
arachnid aplomb   in site waits
it out   weights it
at an edge.

Toddler

1.

Nate in the field
feeling the grass
is that.

2.

In the field—air's
still—the long hair
of cattle doesn't riffle—
are we watching too well?

Ommatidia Song

The sun grows its candor
     in spring until each worker
bee arrives
     with her 5500 lenses in each eye!

11,000 chances to sight the best sips,
     and when she does she spins and tips,
dancing the directions then
     into the splendor of the Open.

A Jar

of black olives
shriveled in
brine—convo-

luted ruts to
the tongue:
each bitter

nipple an
odd Braille of
the withered

countryside
and the blind
pit within.

For Cathy & Bruce

Across Country

At what distance
brother do you wake
now from childhood?

Hammock

To
sway
with
no more self
than dew
on
these
ropes.

Orchard

Now only
the sun

plucks.

Leaves Meaning Leaves

As
if the
flares of fall
intend beyond
color and even
hear we live—as if
we are here only if
we are here to

t
h
e
m

"Waking Up the Rake"

Raking the brilliant slum
of autumn—letting
the rake move in.

Transfer Station

We're slipping empty bottles
into barrels near paper placed
in bins and secrets sealed in plastic

as gossip keeps its mud wet and slung
as every moral compass spins

and the unknown's compacted for the long haul.

Eyeing the Seeds

Just that thin
disc of ice in
the seed bucket

left outside
(my mistake)
overnight

and two
juncos
ice fishing.

How Else?

To be the horizon of a snowflake
setting on your cheek—how

simple, even silly. But to feel
something so delicate in fade, some

thing of the air among the others
and intricate, some thing just itself

once.

As Ancient Romans Thought of Nature

Mourning dove—

voice
portable as despair

we thought you were
only a bird.

==============

Spruce
full of snow—

fog at
branches—

sadness clinging
in spite of you.

February

Beyond the pass

    of small animals whose lives

are snow

    the sound of beech

leaves rattling their winter

    color of salmon—

hanging on.

Power Outage

Old horse wearing snow
    steps into the doorway
        of a dark barn.

Owl sounds *you too, too soon.*

You, too, too soon—as a struck
    match held up
        in the darkness,

into it. Through.

Pogonip

Thick icy fog pine cone hanging being self I call master!

Coyote

Listen
soon the young will follow

elders to the edge
of song

be led to the same wild
movement a branch

of the family
at deer.

March

Old distaff loom mayhap—tension
     of warp with weft—teal scarf
woman below doors-decorating-ceiling
     of this store at hoary end of winter.

Looking up at knobs—she rises
     dances
          cracked
floorboards
        singing.

"In seed time learn,
in harvest teach,
in winter enjoy."

–William Blake

First
day of Spring
and it feels like ten
birds learn from one
bud how to open
song.

Another Springtime Future

No mate yet for the Snowy
Owl on our jasmine green

car roof—or
                (we guess)
for the Dusky Grouse on the lek—

no one's flying—all strut
as magic locks in another's charm.

Humility

As a flea on bedrock tries to sense blood
poet you may have started

to get through to more life as life tries
to get through to you:

there is no rock only this dog
of the world you are riding

About the Author

DAVID GIANNINI's most recently published collections of poetry include *FACES SOMEWHERE WILD, THE FUTURE ONLY RATTLES WHEN YOU PICK IT UP,* and *IN A MOMENT WE MAY BE STRANGELY BLENDED,* all published by Dos Madres Press in 2017, 2018 and 2019; *POROUS BORDERS* published by Spuyten Duyvil Press in 2019; *SPAN OF THREAD* (Cervena Barva Press, 2015) and *AZ TWO* (Adastra Press,) a "Featured Book" in the 2009 Massachusetts Poetry Festival. His work appears in national and international literary magazines and anthologies, including *New Hungers for Old: One-Hundred Years of Italian-American Poetry.* He was nominated for a Pushcart Prize in 2015. New Feral Press published15 of his chapbooks between 2011-18 including *TRAVELING CLUSTER*, and *INVERSE MIRROR*, a collaboration with artist, Judith Koppel. Awards include: Massachusetts Artists Fellowship Awards; The Osa and Lee Mays Award For Poetry; an award for prosepoetry from the University of Florida; and a 2009 Finalist Award from the Naugatuck Review. He has been a gravedigger; beekeeper; taught at Williams College, The University of Massachusetts, and Berkshire Community College, as well as preschoolers and high school students, among others. Giannini was the Lead Rehabilitation Counselor for Compass Center, which he co-founded as the first rehabilitation clubhouse for severely and chronically mentally ill adults in the northwest corner of Connecticut. **www.davidgiannini.com**

COMMENTS ON SOME OF DAVID GIANNINI'S BOOKS:

On *IN A MOMENT WE MAY BE STRANGELY BLENDED*

Giannini's poems are a perfect antidote to the humorless, self-important troubles thrust upon Nature's once simple, now befuddled, plan for the incremental happiness of our species—not. Instead read Giannini for the marvelous fun of it.

—Dennis Daly

On *THE FUTURE ONLY RATTLES WHEN YOU PICK IT UP*

The Future Only Rattles When You Pick It Up is one of a kind. There is nothing like it, and no one's voice or thought is like his. Witty, wise and wonderful, some of these poems are downright hilarious. I won't say which, because it's more fun if you discover them for yourselves. Every once in a while, though, he looks out at us from the page and tells us a bold truth straight on, without humor but with infinite understanding of himself and his place in the world. It isn't until halfway through that we learn where the clever title comes from. I won't spoil it by telling you, except that it's a romantic surprise. My other favorites: "Maysong Other," Parts 1 and 2,"B.A.D.,""Betsy" and the suite of poems

63

for his wife, Pam – especially the 7th, where he says,"…"we are present to each other   the way our talk is   the way our talking is a form a form of being of being present of feeling our talk inlaid inlaid with silence …." The spaces are deliberate, as they are on his page. Anyone picking up this book, whether it rattles or not, is in for an absorbing, delightful and insightful read.

—Irene Willis,
–Editor of the anthology *Sigmund Freud in Poetry*
and Poetry Editor of *International Psychoanalysis*

The Future Only Rattles When You Pick It Up, swerves delightfully through an engaging series of lyrically intense meditations on contemporary American life. Giannini's subject matter ranges from the human genome to the continental divide, from his father's wristwatch ticking in his casket to an erasure of a Petrarchan sonnet, from Ars Poetica to love poem to philosophical assay and back again. These poems, visually and aurally acrobatic, provide evidence of a subtle and wildly imaginative intelligence. Giannini is a poet at the height of his powers, whose work skitters on the verge of unknowing, but always refracts a certain slant of revelatory light.   —Dante Di Stefano, Ph.D.,

Best American Poetry.com

On *FACES SOMEWHERE WILD*

David Giannini's *Faces Somewhere Wild* spans his 45 years living and laboring in the Berkshire hill-towns of Massachusetts. Like the farmer whose *face resembles what's fixed and moves around him*, he is an astute observer of other faces. The man-with-the-broom who walks the streets making sweeping gestures reminds the poet, *We are becoming motes or star dust*. This resonates with the cosmic pedigree of the fallen drunk by the roadside: *I drink the ancient atoms from a cask*. Old Jane *sees her dead daughter is a whitetail doe*. The poet tracks the faces he sees for traces of the *original faces somewhere wild*, the revelation of *something you were before all else, /something you were before all this*. Giannini is the poet-hunter, who identifies himself as prey, in search of what waits at the threshold of expression: I*t wants to grab you by the throat. You don't turn away; /instead, you unbutton your shirt*. Even as he fleshes the world with words, the poet strips it back to a superordinate mystery of *atoms in super positions/in two or more planes at once*. Giannini makes no attempt to resolve the paradox. Our guide through the Berkshires renders the vessel of creation as both full and empty. *Feeling emptiness wing into you with its terror! Then owl to the empty nest. No reason not to have wept. Faces Somewhere Wild* is a perch where the burden of mortality touches our hearts. Highly recommended.

—Paul Pines

On *SPAN OF THREAD*

David Giannini's "Span of Thread," which is a polyphonic, se-
rio-playful, deep-structured celebration of life-in-language and
language-in-life. This book is further proof that Giannini is
among those who are saving American poetry from itself.

—Joseph Hutchison,
Poet Laureate of Colorado

"Span of Thread" is masterful, sinking the needle of Giannini's
genius deep into the wonder of all things.   —Leo Seligsohn,
former critic for *Newsday.*

On *POROUS BORDERS*

In his latest collection, David Giannini works the "porous bor-
ders" between poetry and prose, tragedy and whimsy, gravity
and absurdity, to offer up a grab bag of playful, thought-pro-
voking pleasures that are "something more than real" but rather
"meta-real, hyper-real, surreal, irreal," as befits a world in which
"the real thing . . . is always at least partly a drafty, shifty, get-
my-drift, daffy alembic grab-bag, wifty and makeshift." Not so
these verbal gems, whose fancy and fantasy enriches their reso-
nance in an alchemy akin to "light tr[ying] to shed from a dark

place to golden itself" or those answers "behind every door . . . eavesdrop[ping] on the deft noise of questions" which we hadn't realized were troubling us, until encountering this unique and delightful book   —Susan Lewis,

editor of *Posit*, author of *Heisenberg's Salon*

In these vertical prose poems, Porous (more Stevens's Crispin than Berryman's Henry) takes us through condensed narratives to grand myth and philosophy. Correspondence here leads to contradiction: "each is a shutter of the other." And along the way devilish angels offer "another place, also of poetry, a place of lyric dissociation, a locus" on the page -- these "micro-monoliths" swirl with macro-spin.   — Dennis Barone

On *RIM/WAVE*

This beautiful book is actually two books in one. Rim is the fictional account of the title character, a farmhand who both lives and works within the harshness of the physical world, and who sees beyond it to the spiritual and the metaphysical. Whether we call this a prose poem or a story told in the language of poetry, this is a powerful narrative of a character I won't soon forget. The story is further enhanced by representations of woodcuts by Franklin Feldman. The second part of this impressive work is a collection of poems called *To the Wave, Poetry at Seacoasts*. In these poems Giannini reflects on people he has loved, and on the earth, water, and air of and around the ocean and the animals that inhabit that space. Many of these poems, though short, resonate deeply, and few poets get so much from so few words. These two books complement each other through Giannini's great skill with language and his ability to join the concrete and the abstract. It's poetry grounded in the earth.

—Mark Farrington,
Director of M.A. in Writing and Teaching Writing Programs,
The Johns Hopkins University, Washington, D.C. and Baltimore, MD.

On *OTHERS' LINES*

I don't see how any close reader won't come away learning a great deal about the potential in quotation, the distinctness of first lines & the possibilities of form. That's a lot for a project of this scope to accomplish.   —Ron Silliman

To draw on others' lines so neatly and discreetly and wisely and well is a rare feat and one anyone can savor who opens this charming chapbook.   —Cid Corman

Yes, it's very deftly done, and there is much that is both attractive and amusing: Paul Pines, Charles Olson, and Howard Nemerov as bedfellows is a bit difficult to imagine, but your result is convincing. What comes through to me is the likenesses between all human beings, no matter how differently they may perceive things. It certainly must have been a colossal undertaking.   —Theodore Enslin

I think you have really triumphed. These are poems that succeed most of the time as poetry and carry a real spiritual impact. And your way of using the whole page, if necessary, to get the space/ time equivalents you need may transform all of our writing.

— Robin Magowan

On *STEM*

These poems know a mysterious grace. They hover lightly about the imminent birth of things, taking shape from the clenching & declension of the story locked in the human form. The human they propose is a sum of the covert intelligence of the world when it "works", an ear minutely attuned to the folding * unfolding of creation. Flight, grace, transparency is how they tread, bending neither the grass nor the flowers that *inch out /*

lean against gravity. As Guillevic said, they do to light what light does to them.   — Andrei Codrescu

David Giannini is one of the most interesting and original of American poets.   —James Laughlin

OTHER BOOKS BY DAVID GIANNINI
PUBLISHED BY DOS MADRES PRESS

FACES SOMEWHERE WILD - 2017
THE FUTURE ONLY RATTLES WHEN YOU PICK IT UP - 2018
IN A MOMENT WE MAY BE STRANGELY BLENDED - 2019

FOR THE FULL DOS MADRES PRESS CATALOG:
www.dosmadres.com